# Heat Signature

# Heat Signature

*Siobhán Campbell*

Seren is the book imprint of
Poetry Wales Press Ltd.
57 Nolton Street, Bridgend, Wales, CF31 3AE
www.serenbooks.com
facebook.com/SerenBooks
twitter@SerenBooks

ISBN: 978-1-78172-367-8
ebook: 978-1-78172-368-5
Kindle: 978-1-78172-369-2

A CIP record for this title is available from the British Library.

The publisher acknowledges the financial assistance of the Welsh Books Council.

Cover Image: 'Flaming Flowers' © Frieda Hughes

Printed by Airdrie Print Services Ltd

# Contents

I

# The shame of our island

is that we killed the wolf.
Not just the last
but the two before that.

I knew a man who met a man
who was the cousin removed
of the great-grandson of the man
who killed the third-last wolf
on the island.

Slit it he did,
to see the steaming innards –
how long they were, how tightly wound.

Had it a white paw to the fore?
That gene would have been recessive.
Was there a black bar across the yellow eye?
No time to notice its *différence*.

Is this a wolf with its bared teeth
and its lairy smell
and its fetlock tipped with white?

Is this wolfish?

# Tone

Tone says here is the other cheek, why don't you have a go at that?
Tone is when you're giggling at a double bluff and you see someone crying.
Tone is an artist dropping a Ming vase and calling that *art*. Tone is another
artist slashing that guy's canvas, calling him a fart. Tone is muscling up to
the Peace People, they don't have a mandate for peace. Tone sings a Satanic
mass in the civic centre, where tone agrees to use vinegar for urine.
Tone is an author in search of a character able to roll tone home from the bank.
Tone wants a reader in tune with the tone that is there and the one that is not.
Tone is peeling an orange in its pocket so the smell will madden, building
a bungalow on your eyelid with an overlook to the back. Tone is a weasel,
drawing the birds down with a special sensuous dance and then, tone is lunch.

Nothing trumps tone but when there's a crack in it, watch what slips in.
It might be an anti-tone – undoing bravura, dulling the gloss, leaving tone spent,
in a fierce bad mood, exposed in the light of all that we once thought we shared.

# Weeding

When you weed a field, bend over the long root suckers,
the weeders moving in a line across the ridges,
a stippled human stripe of inclined heads against
the ordered rippling rows of mangels,
then the world seems right and we are in our place.

When you refuse to weed and hang out with a friend
under the dreeping willow in the bend that is not ploughed
where no grass grows over the stones and what is buried,
you watch the workers easing themselves to night,
its shadow keeps ahead of them as they cross.

Then you might think of sacrifice or the greater good
but you don't, flirty with heat as heat leaves the day
and you separate, seeing things anew, filthy
with possibility. It's too late now to join the weeding crew.
And the willow laughs its long thin laugh at you.

# Photos of the islanders

They have forebears. Noses and foreheads
forged in the art of fact.
They have seen a daughter wither from ill use,
prayed for her, sent bread to her funeral.

There's a welcome stapled to their tongue
and they count your leavings when you're gone.
      *What we make now must get us through the winter.*

What do they see when they look out –
a one who says they are still married to belief,
a one who thinks they are mired in a falsehood?

Is the split at the picture edge
an implication? That they neither do
nor undo.

★

*Poverty Isolation Tradition*
Pressure comes in threes.
Devout in practice, loved by an unnamed god,
who will they be today?

Who will they be today?
Masked by the strip of archetype.
Life as a scene of foreshadows.

★

He wears the dagger tattoo of his father
and his cap, and like him can
twist his eyes into his head
leaving the whites behind.

Losses eddy in lines about the mouth
and when he sits, because his father asks
to help repair the trawl,
he is tamed in the fray of its knots.

★

A line of men along a wall
each of them matched by a pine behind.
They sit and the dry wall presses back
a heritable skill, plucking and picking
by sight and feel. Wall-making by touch.

One has a hat with ribbon bands,
the dandy among them –
equally protected and despised.

They share the hill behind until they die
thinking it is theirs.

★

clearing stones the first peoples made the fields
and on nights with a red dusk you can hear them ease
the pain of strained backs, too much bend
how three feet takes a whole night to clear
how the wall begins at the edge with what they sling
the wall begins to keep something in

if you follow a heifer she will show you where there's a spring
of fresh water
not everything is old wives' tales

★

just what would fill the head of a goat
we know the fleet of its feet
the bass of its baa
the burr on its coat

when we know the fleet of its feet
the burr of its baa
the bass of its burr
how to turn on a goat
look it square in the eyes
the dare of it

disrespect in the pupil

it can be slit before its hoary time
the flat black capsule of the pupil

slit and hung before its hoary time
how to better a goat
we've passed this down

the only way is to make a pipe we play
from the sac of its udder
then blow a melody out of her

a mournful lament is the only way
to get the better of a goat

is the way we put a pipe in its udder
    then finger a melody

put in the pipe
    put in the pipe and squeeze a music from the teats

# 'In their high cheek bones run the veins of a nation'

Characters choose to resemble the noble peasant.
They look as if they know the value of elbow grease.
Even though their backs are bent with longing,
they may appear taller than they are.

One might willingly tell of the devil, sitting there on her left,
making her write with the wrong, giving Teacher such a fright
he brought the strap down *Whack*. Tied the offending hand
behind her back. Now she's ambidextrous.

Some may say they lived through the Famine,
or at least were sent packing west of the river
where they told stories set by fires in one-roomed schools
and caressed the oppressor's tongue.

In this genre, beware of a creeping nostalgia.
Nothing grows resentment better than an acre of stones.
An island passport might land you a tax haven.
Then again it could cost you an arm and a leg.

# Piebald

Horses of the others,
the thinkers, the travellers,
tethered on the edge of new dual carriageways,
tied in the blank side of advance factories.
They verge on the flanks of dealers and shakers
where plans end in a thicket of rubble and stumps.
What are they for?

A yelled canter down the scruff-sides of dusty villages,
barebacked warmth sidling
and a hearts-beating thud between your knees –
where mis-remembrance is a dream to nourish,
where promise can out-run irony.
Not the hero horses, beauties black and brave,
who took the warrior to battle and will not return,
these are compromised, misled and confused,
heads too big for their ribcage, scrawny as the
screed of grass they pull.

Yet they must have been there from the start –
round the back of wired-off ruminations.
We pretended not to notice the occasions
when they recalled a field,
the hock-stripping speed of a gallop down a long hedge
where a quiver of legends misted into song.
But when they started to gather
in places built to house a desperation,
they seemed to trick our vision of a freedom.

That was a world we lost before it named us —
none of the promise, the clang
of potential,
instead the fetters that hold us to self-interest
the binds that make taxes out of failure.
That was a world lost before we named it,
part of a larger undertaking
to help us understand captivity.
*Go back, go back* they seem to say
but we have no direction,
rounding again the ring road to the city
as if we know the story behind the story.

# Republica dolorosa

I didn't mean it personally. Not as a fanatic strips a thousand year old Icon with a knife because they are alone with it in a darkened room and it beckons. Not like that. I didn't mean to do it, wobbling a path down the garden with an over-full wheel barrow to sever the bee as big as a knuckle, smack in the middle of the crazy paving. I thought it was dead already. But the bees came, swung their severed force at me, their world wrecker. Upways, edgeways and every-ways; virgins, workers and drones, all forgetting the sworn dance. Not in swarm but in confusion. Confusion, as if they know how things have ravelled out, how we hate majesty, the daring of it, pushed in our proletarian faces. Apparently I dared to kill a queen. Now I operate outside the protocols, not knowing who is on the inside track, realising the barrow is upset, the flood gates are open; we are standing on the brink of the slippery slope. When the icon is sooth-slashed, who will teach us how to cope?

# Interference

I'm on a caffeine high and on the street and on the steps
and in the crowded train, everybody seems their loveliest,
their best selves hauled out of beds, scrubbed, finished with
a comb, moisture still glistening in their pores. I could hug
them all and I'm one of them, all business this day with
work to go to and a bag full of scripts to mark. My coffee
is the free one you get after eight others and the barista
says *regular skinny cappuccino* and it tastes all the smoother
from someone who could have been a friend, judging from
her sparky shoulders.

       *Announcement: Southern Rail is delayed
due to a person under train.* Briefly, with a smidgen of doubt,
I see the brain opened by speed, the steel cauliflower-slice before
the blood but then a tiny infant in a blue suit smiles half at me
and I catch his eye and we play peek-a-boo around my cup.

Could this be a church really, right here on the morning train,
could this be church? And thank god, or that beyond which
there is no appeal for the bean growers and the harvesters,
the roasters and the drivers that bring this treasure
from Colombia (certain other cargoes in slip-sided vents);
the middle men and women, all just trying to raise their kids
and give them an education – except those that are not. And I
think of the last time I was in church before the cardinal said
that it was right in canon law for that priest to do nothing
after children were raped except tell his superior, tell his superior
and skip back to the sacristy to get sacramental. It was right
in Canon Law.

       And it's clear that law is not what these lovelies
want, nor what I want nor what the dote in the blue suit wants.
How can they not see that we are holy? Is it that holding
things in place long enough to enter your pores renders a question
that halves itself on the way from right to left brain and halves again
until it's in so many pieces you can hardly bear to keep them but
you know it can go on halving? And why did that person, heart
scudding, wrist pulsing, walk out under that train this morning?

# Lace

Crochet, a hook and one set of fingers
curling and coiling a hesitant confection
in thread that will stand up on its own.
Not lace but lacy, the effort
scrunching up your face, the making
of making in your short-sighted eye.
Potential. How before you begin,
it is clambering clean and forever.
You seem to detach from the chair
from the room from the world we are in
when you pull intent out of air.
Might it be a welcome, set under two glasses
of scotch on a bedside table? Might it be
a collar laid over yoke like a nun's
from a convent in France? Could it
muster charity while calling
the willing eye to prayer? They told you
lace that is not lace will not seduce.
You smooth a medieval dark down
through its gaps, stemming the curlicue
loop, its interweaving.
The twist of a flaw, that disappointment,
how not to use it, *the better to strengthen
the whole*, that would be cliché,
and this is lace if not yet lacy.

# The Lease

The widow was protected
by every cancer, liver or lung
by the heifer found hung
by poison in the well
by gypsies and their tell
by the lawyer in his seat
who rounded down instead of up
by the grant giver
the inspector's cover,
all that holds things in together
so they seem, they seem
until the widow's curse is slated
her lease is not renewed
and we know next to nothing
about what might be lost
until the day they roll their tools
into her yard, to strip her pipes
and prise her roof apart.

# The longing of the bees

Gather together, whisper into the ferns, send a trill
out with the mistle thrush. What we have to learn
is that they must be heard. If they arrive all at once
to remind us of a plague, mutant in their anger,
loud in their sway, then we might be persuaded,
even while netting drains, sealing the gaps in outer doors.

Be ready to puncture that inner ear, it is no longer
needed. Brace yourself for commotion. A brouhaha
if ever you saw one. Tumult of absence, uproar of lack.
Without them it seems, nothing is fertile; wheat becomes
an illusion, oil will not press from seeds that were not crossed.

Who knew the workers had a feel for dork and drone?
Castrati singing in our ears while we sweltered,
checking our influence in waves of disproportion.
Research shows that genes are not the problem.
We resolve to put a capsule into space, a narrative
for those who may yet come. Listen to the hedges
it will say. Remember, to swarm is not to warn.

# Warrenpoint

I was born after the event. In the undergrowth
we ate liquorice leaves, blackened our tongues
so we could say bad words like *cunt*.
We talked to the bogey man who lived in the wood.
He went hatless and hunching to the convent door
every day save Friday when they dipped fish.
The roads ended in hills where the world began.
When the sun went down it lit up other people's lives.
If we wanted a goose we went to the goose farm,
chased them until they were solid with fear.

In the summer we swapped nest eggs.
That we laughed was no guarantee of hatching.
We played soccer in a field flattened out of a hill,
our balls scuppered on pricks of thistle-down.
*Exponential* was a word I learned from the radio
bringing the maimings close.
Our attics linked up if you wall-crawled through.
From the last window we could watch the street unreel.

# Periwinkles

Long after pollution was confirmed, you insisted
on picking periwinkles by the Bull Wall.
We swapped them in the kitchen for fresh ones
from Thomas's fish stall in Mary Street.
And when you went out door-to-door for Fianna Fáil,
they thought your northern accent helped to swell
the brand of softer nation they were selling.
Dev had been betrayed and those treaty chaps
were led astray, forgetting the sacrifice of the sixteen.
The inheritance was clear, a straight line back
from there to here and a daughter who believed
not one word of it, until you took her up –
gave her the tether tour, backing around
Stranmillis to Malone. That's where Muldoon slipped
out a window of a night to meet his squeeze.
And there's the bay those giant roses set alight.

# Convexed

If the eye of Ireland is really Lough Neagh,
is it all-seeing or blinkered down one side?
Does it know the difference between reed beds
and seedy edges, bulrush and sedge way?
Can it feel the scoring of oars on nights
with a black finish or tell when small
little stones are pulled by more than a boat?
Looking up, possibly through us, the lake
feels huge in its land bed as if we could never
know it as scooped from the hand of Fionn
or as pissed from the horse of Aengus.
And if it looks down, is there a swirl from
the eddies, a sucking out of capillaries
as every last drop down to the centre of that
inexplicable body of water slips through
the upholdings of the expert water leveller?

# Framed

Because he had a large growth on his neck they called him
Dinny of the unborn twin and the worst of them asked
if he ever voted for labour. When the ships came in
there were containers to lift with the new-fangled thing-uma-
jig that took away the jobs of fourteen dockers. Once
a smallish wooden pallet that got sent the wrong way from
Guyana. Pineapples, smelling to high heaven. The scent of
the Caribbean, though we argued about whether Guyana
was South American or part of the Anglo-Carib proper.
Sparks who had BBC World Service said it was; he'd heard
a long-boat-man from there tell how they roasted coconuts
on fires till they burst with the heat of their milk, making a
splatter that they ate all up, washed off the stickiness in
the tide. But there was a reason to begin this… yes, the
question of the unborn and the rights of same. Well, we
brought Dinny in, all scrubbed up, to the minister. Frame
was his name, from somewhere down west where they've
those long towns built toward the worship hall and they're
trained to stare straight and to think straight. Reverend,
we said, there's a growing boy out the back of this man's neck
and we think, as you are the upstanding and the outstanding
you should now stand up for the rights of the yet to be born
and get it out for us, yes, get it out. Well, he's still looking at us
with one eye forlorn as a burnt out tree and the other whipped
clean to the whiskey. We turned him that day it's true as god,
and he left for Scotland once the spring came in and didn't even
have a farewell do for his leaving. Somewhere in the outer or the
inner Hebrides they say, there's a squinter of a man who was
once of the cloth and his crossing is and his crossing was and
his crossing always will be forever and ever

# Ravens

Ravens in their *ruaile buaile* hear the tick of season-tuning trees
they colonise like something moral to be despised.
Out of the regions of the tourist dark they surprise by being
here, by being real. I am aware that our language crosses swords.
Your capped heads, your jagged faces, not all one colour, no,
you are blue and grey gradations, you are indigo inked to the red
edge. The stones you drop crack open a rival's eggs.

There is a smite of forever in the calluses behind your beak
though some of you ail and moult and cheep rather than caw.
You are not omens of something happening elsewhere, petty deaths
on the other side of the hill nor votes casting a future of transaction,
a tit for tat, a blind eye bought for less than it cost last year.
Lone selves, nothing as trite as foretelling in your congregation.

How to approach you, how to be in the same acre? How not to ask
why you screech now, wheeling over the trees, or why you quieten,
each staking yourselves out. You do this. You show aspiration up
and dress it down. Are you most apt for how little is known?
This is not wild. This is not idle. Ravens have said it all, almost.
Here comes the horseman, may I say 'pass by'?

# Interviewing the beast

My mother is Sappho, my father is Homer, she told me.

*I lived with the real things of the earth. If you go to bed*
*with wet hair you will wake up with meningitis.*

The tea leaves recounted her past in five different ways.
One where King Billy was vanquished, there were no apprentice boys,
no secret societies save those led by the pope.

*If you cut down an oak, the tree peoples will colonise your head.*
*I have lived with the double-jointed tongue of Fionn.*
*Where he needed friends, he tied it to the roof of his mouth.*
*When he wanted a rout, he released it to greet his enemy.*

Once when she was little, there was a statue that moved, bent from the hip
in a green grotto at night. They all thought it a sign but she knew of people
pulling lights this way and that, acting for things beyond.
Using your tendency against you, I said. I didn't record my nods.

*When there are red berries in a month with no r, the world has slipped*
*on its axis, a splinted angle not to be measured as if matter.*

In one scenario she speaks in tongues, thinking it lowland Gaelic,
adding consonants to vowels, coughing up phlegm.
Not the real thing but a story that implies it: this is her method.

*When we look at the fields, they curl at the edges, showing the layers of greed.*
*To seek an assistant, I strike a match to the face.*

*Blow it out, you are hired.*

# The water level

Snow water I've never had,
but hear that it can freeze
the lumbar of your brain,
leave you able to do long division.

Cabbage water though, I've tried.
Greener than cut grass,
a smell of iron to turn your stomach,
bits of bacon fat floating in it.

Trough water to wash that down
filtered through drainpipe and drip flute,
seeped taste of their mongering
swilled to the old tin trough.

The softest sweetest rain is here
this side of the mountain,
drops its sediments beyond
and only brings us pure clear water
fit for gods.

# Drumlins have no personality

they bland the land,
make one space much like another.
The road imposed by tar
could ribbon off at any moment –
pop open a corpuscle, a sup-hole of slippage.

In the dips between shale hills
is water or its suggestion.
The glands of a fish were found here
petrified in a granite slate.

If you could find where it ends,
this is egg-in-a-basket topography,
undulations for a giant game of hide and seek,
threnody for straw boys
and those who chase the wren.

In the few straggling bushes,
polished pockets of stasis.
What would it be to sink here
if these hills reversed,
plug holes to a swipe of earth?

They cannot be farmed. They will not be domestic.

They ask for nothing
but leave us a little frantic,
a touch of babble at the edges of our springs.

# Drip Feed

The trough beside the house is thick
with dashed hopes. There before brick,
before mortar, for travelling horses, stages
from their posts, its sides poured and patted
keep the mark of spade and blade, spit
in its mottled pocks and fear of the ganger.

This is the drowning spot for runts of litters,
sow's disgrace squealing down the night,
when straw runs short and tempers fester envy.
Here birds fall, the souls of angels trapped
in slow-flapped deaths though no-one ventures
why in heaven's name they failed to fly.

But it's the cat, set on the aspic shelf
that stays wet to the touch. Rigor bound
with four trip-rigid legs. Cat in its drowned
death no longer Tabby, but something more dead,
more of a shock to find in the wide morning
of visitor delight than any reminder
that we know nothing yet.

II

# Concentration

What are things made of?
The scrape of the potty from under the bed
would wake the dead. My grandaunt's squat
of balance as she aims, hitching a flannel nightdress
high enough to miss its faded pinkness.

Back into bed lighter, pot pushed under,
a yellow fresh smell like a shape in the room.
Steam must be rising from both sides beneath us.
If we were taken, assumed, we would be ready,
be-calmed, made holy by the body.

Her King Charles spaniels with Venetian
glass eyes look on from either end of the mantle.
Forever apart in painted disdain, making space
actual between them. The pride of one
is trumped by the wink of the other.

When things attract our deep attention
they give back out the stare that we put in.
We know this is commitment of relation.
And though it seems innocent to say,
it is a form of love.

# Chink

I dare not move before our baby wakes
in case we lose these last moments of doze.
You have your morning tic, a click-jaw
loud enough to wake even the daws that nest
in our bedroom chimney stack. The room shrinks
to your impending clack and my full nose, waiting
for a sneeze. We're fixed, long enough to look once
at each other, each a sleep-drooled, chosen lover.
Our toes graze, by accident we think, a touch
we will not gauge till later. I break, reach
for a tissue, notice that we have open peepers.
This, the first time she wakes without a cry.
She has become the keeper of our gaze,
her look, where we begin and end our days.

# The Blessing

How we nearly met our deaths on that bend –
watching his cassock and surplice,
the white of his collar against the black;
how he offered to give us his first blessing,
just ordained that hour with no-one to celebrate,
he was giving his outfit a walk on the roads.

We knelt, what else could we do?
His voice held the yearn of the ages,
threat of a gift we could not refuse.
It told of mass rocks and penal laws
the power of dissolving marriages
the fourth secret of Fatima.

We knelt to feel that life was serious,
though our fishing rods awaited and the flies
we tied that morning might be wilting,
though lake shadow would be moving fish
toward the bank where weeds
would reach right up to catch our lines.

We knelt and felt the power of his illusion;
he might have been talking to his lonely self,
counting things that tie him to the world,
no inheritance, but a scattering of Latin,
and a sense of the largeness of the arguments.

When he lifted a white hand, so clean
and clear was that hand that it drew
a world as it moved, a rise and fall
in it like a boat on a spring swell.
We didn't hear a word he said.

Just at Amen, the ford transit van hurtled
round the corner and we leapt, sprang
from kneeling, jumped clear into the hedge,
scratches on our hands, thorns
in our sweaters, the cleric akimbo.

We nearly met our deaths,
but maybe we were ready
as ready as we'll ever be
given his first blessing.

# Fodder

What you have seen cornfield, could make you weep.
The stories they tell from the north
would be worthless to yours.
When you were a battleground, you held your whist.
One side or another, whoever won would need to eat.
You have ears to hear the centuries whisper
but mostly you heed your own low murmur –

Cornfield, when the breeze flies through you,
makes a set dance of your bright tips,
or when a path opens up to your centre
as if a mysterious finger parts your waves,
then we could believe you hold the wisdom of the ages.
But you might not agree.
You might say instead,
*Just believe in corn.*

## Clifden 1984

Coming from the city to the land of black armbands
I did not dare to ask the question of the day.
Hammerhead knew it, drowned in his knowing.
They found him puffed to his enormous brow.

Out here the sun will leave only when pushed.
Down into the sea it goes, setting the night creatures free.
Walking Sky Road leads to thoughts that fly apart
and will not be re-hooked.

Everyone knows the Dutchman who swims naked in snare cove.
His purple cock swings into the dreams of peeping girls.
*No surrender, Ulster says no; Out out out; the lady's not for turning.*

We, who were never Catholic before,
are reading the new covenant of liberation.
Sound-bites from Peru excite our tongues.

The summer is long enough to wait for new translations.
When they re-sit, they may reframe the question.
We try growing beards, not shaving our legs,
practice mantras as if we could go mystic in the morning.

# War has been given a bad name

*(after Brecht)*

I am told that the best people have begun to say,
from a moral point of view, how it is difficult now
to believe in a cause. With international terror, the
homegrown sort was difficult to ignore. Of course
the finest of us were never in their target, being able
to justify the conflict for either side. But even the bishop
is concerned about absolution: perhaps a collective
blessing where nobody catches his eye. Business types
warn about recession, as most of those 'volunteers'
will need a pension. Some even think it better to maintain
status quo. But they do say we should attend the *Let go
and Forget* sessions, coupons free with national newspapers.
I believe they have someone there so mesmerising that even
those with holes through their palms may learn to pray.

# Origin of the mimeo

What do guns when they are not in use?
In the dead of night they double and divide,
naming new owners, finding a new ruse.

Carry a gun on stage, it must be fired.
*Deterrent* only lasts until undone.
Better they are counted out of mind.

List the ways to frame a decommission,
a car-park graveyard covered with cement.
Which stay on stasis is sufficient?

Marking each as *put beyond use*.
Keeping their provenance as you would art.
Rocking the replicas back to their false start.
It's got to be efficient.

# Learning Greek in Knockanes

Whiff of dead cow from a lorry's lurch.
Out to be out, one solitary walker,
I hope to go as far as the garden centre
where half a loaf is hung from the Laburnum.

No low wall to sit from here to there,
just these quick grow hedges, leafing fast
to mask the hangers of inverted temples,
many fine archways for the bats.

Cobwebs have ionised the monkey puzzle
where birds insist on calling out a summer.
And look, a jogger getting smaller and thinner
runs himself on into the damp.

The ranch house waits for its seventh pillar,
gapes at a sun room, massively blank.
Peonies nustle in a stone swan's back
tickling those wings about to flap.

Pruned garnish, an island on the gravel,
nothing edible for anyone outcast.
But two eagles prepare on cement posts
to guard against whatever might be worse.

A vacant site, bullocks breathe the gap
before new earth movers arrive.
Yellow tabs jammed in their jet ears
catch the last inkling of the light.

The jogger's back, damp-dark in his vest,
incoming rain glistening on his legs.
I'd best turn round, head into the mist
from halfway to where I meant to get.

# Climb

the mountainy men toward the top
are tiny on the outcrop
can they see us wave
from our nice café
where we wait for their pride

do they know that we watched
a bad-tempered cloud threaten
to squall and haul them soggy and shaky
down early until

some other hill took the damp
and they carried on up with their ropes
harnesses, hope and flasks
to the top or nearly

where they are now, they could touch it
a ridge that's measured in inches
and even sixteenths matter when you
gauge a mountain for climbing

though not to us, as we sip
our hot chocolate, glancing up
now and then to make sure
we're not needed

# Clew Bay from the Reek

No way to pace yourself or plan a rest.
Each ridge peak declares itself a fake.
So on, over fences of chicken net
that mark out fields of sheep dropping and rock.
We may be on the wrong side of the stack.
Each patch is someone's care but we are glad
to find some sagging wire, paths worn down
by pilgrims; like us, not the barefoot kind.
At last the top. A tough stone chapel
and a saint's hard bed. And look, the cloud
beneath breaks open to begin a bay,
blue and green as earth seen from our
nearest star, perfect as paint. Panting
we count the islands in its keep, one
for each day of the year, though some tiny,
just a nest, a pair of gannets maybe—
not that we can see them from up here but
think, and of the salt clams beneath
clamping cool suckers to the planted rocks
or oysters, growing their cold pearl hearts
where even now a stone might lodge to rub
itself into a keepsake of love. Pots of lobster,
meat of the sea, boiled from life, slathered in
butter as a feast; all this we see
and separate out from our group to feel
how things are shifting from this height,
how we're lifted out of ourselves until one,
young and without fear, begins to whoop
a clear, felt sound, a rare high tremor.
She whoops and waves her arms as if to take
it all, gather in against whatever comes—
false ridges that may yet hide proper peaks,
she whoops and whoops for every one of us
and how we are discovered by a reek.

# Flora

The cow is on top of her game,
her haunches fat, her bones rounded.
She feels the goddess power of her udder
in the mould-damp dark of the milking shed.

If she stays still, all may be well.
If she thinks of the cool absence of horns,
feels their undead weight balancing her head,
she may contain herself.

But if she kicks the bucket at full froth,
tips it from the milker's raw-red hand –
then she begins a hell which gathers heat
all through the livelong days without that milk.

# Uncle Paddy and the man from Atlantis

After devotions, Paddy took his stick and wandered down the strand. Seagulls were not caterwauling for once. He could hear the breeze speak in its foreign tongues of all the places it had been but one place was new. Atlantis the easterly said using the lip of his cap to articulate. Atlantis. It's west of here don't you know and rises in the coil of unset minds.

Now it was crawling dusk and the rocks had that shifty-shape as they prepared to move in the night. Paddy nubbed the sand with his stick so it should stay just where it was and he could see where he'd been if he looked back. Then he saw the man, lolled against a rock gone rose in the sun's deplete, his shoes beside him creased with salt as if they'd been a long time drying by the sea.

Paddy had never met a traveller who would not tell a tale, even if it took until the end of the pouring night and the barrel was in the dregs so no head came on the pint. He sat beside the man. The day crept off the beach onto the water and tripped its way toward that far horizon. I know you are from Atlantis he said to the man, I was told as much. Maybe it's that if you speak you break the spell.

He reached a packet of polo mints out of his pocket and offered it to the man. They sat and ate through the rest of the mints, Paddy having to suck one of them hard to get it off the tooth that had fallen in and the man eating his with a daintiness that Paddy hadn't seen since the wedding breakfast of Myrna on the hill. At last Paddy said, will you tell me your tale?

And the man spoke in a rasp and no accent that was ever heard aloud: you can hear it yourself if you look to where your envy lodges like a jewelled ulcer in your gut, to where the memory of lust in its first rush is livid with longing, to where you have hated your own sister because she was your mother's favourite and got to name the pet lamb.

Paddy must have closed his eyes with the shock of knowing for when he opened them the man was gone and he would never be able to hear the end of the traveller's tale though he looked for him through summer and winter and especially when the seagulls quietened down and the breeze tipped and whittled at his bones –

47

# Camouflage

How many steps back does a soldier take
before he is due to turn around? Long stride.
Short stop. Every gate pillar has potential.
The butcher shop is open today. Fish, fresh
from the lough, hit the counter with a slipped slap.
We are out collecting rubber bullets – pocket money
for the pictures. Internal injuries braised for later.
Watching is too small a word. Desire informs
the way we see them walk. Their tempered dance
is riddled implication. They can turn into a bush
at a given sound. But the foliage is wrong for here.
We know where they are. We want to bring them
tea, hear them try to pronounce our names,
but there's no way of saying this to camouflage.

# The Latest

Our ignorance is out of all proportion.
We try to say the word condolence.
Actors are threading their leaders' voices.
We listen but cannot tell the difference.

We try to say the word condolence.
Pity can make nothing happen.
We listen, but cannot tell the difference.
We even think of envying their passion.

Pity can make nothing happen.
Have words learned to breathe under siege?
We even think of envying their passion,
crediting the rhetoric of either side.

Have words learned to breathe under siege?
What is the meaning of causation?
Crediting the rhetoric of either side,
we're guilty in ways we cannot fathom.

What is the meaning of causation?
We work on an honest confusion.
Guilty in ways we cannot fathom,
careful to make no assumptions.

We work on an honest confusion.
Our ignorance is out of all proportion.
Careful to make no assumptions,
we listen for cues as an actor.

# Colonial Drift

Re-naming the institutions.
Counting the freckles between sleeve and sling.
Watching the mountains change colour in time
to the drums.

Matching ghosts to their namesakes,
licking their like out of bricks.
Dismantling the wall
and re-making it as a cube.

Acting surprised
when plates take off across the room.
How many troubled souls to make a poltergeist?

Re-drawing the districts.
Counting the votes due from each house.
Adding name variations
in three official languages.

Calculating the rate of shift,
taxes due on the living and the dead.

# Why islanders don't kiss hello

And it's not just the bad-timing nose-grazing
jaw against pursed expectation, nor
is it because of Judas
(though he slips out the side door of this discussion)
but more that it seems too familiar
as we have not been to pre-school with your mother.
Perhaps we are not fully of the Europe
where the lean-to nature of a kiss can denote
who will be shafted in a vote.
Or is it just a fear of being wrong, two in
Paris, three in Zagreb and so on?
Right-left instead of left-right could affect the funding
for those new roads in Cavan.
It's not to do with hygiene;
we shake hands happily instead
but we've learned because we must,
being from the island of largesse,
to give that peck of venture in a shared future
where the view over one shoulder is as good
from this side as the other.

## Bog Swimming

Never again we say each year, bitten by midges
into promises we won't keep. Then again
we wonder about the depth. Will the pool hole
hold us in its deep or will drought have shrunk it,
reeds have choked it, bulrushes have blocked it?
A flask is essential, the craw of *Irish* down our gorge.
No one has fenced this bit of bog, recalling some
ancient right of way, some widow's curse
that could get you rightly. A globule of fear
down the slather side of the cut and we're off!
Ease is not sun is not shade. So many things are not
what they appear, yet we have a bog and grog
and wherever there's a might there's a maybe.

# About cows

They shit a lot and at first it is a warm pat
ridged with raised circles as it dries.
Water stopped in its tracks or a viscous jelly
hardening from the outside in.
I think of dying in a pool of shite,
the one my mother meant –
*Go take a running leap in the slurry pit for all I care.*
We had lost three cats that summer.
Seeing them stiffed, legs rigid and shining
made an art of death.
But this was to be about cows,
their lumbering walk to the gap to be milked
as if they know more together than apart.
They can smell a stream of fresh water from a mile.
They can hear grass growing under the bull.
They hold time in their four stomachs, chewing it down
till the evening milking, feeling the hours move on through.
They do not miss the calves they have had taken.
No attachment is apparent in three days.
Perhaps like the farmer in a unit of money,
they count on exchange.
Cows know their own patch but they'll stray to graze another's.
Swung towards the hedge in rain, heads dripping,
tail swatch taking a rest from flies.
Apparently rural but worldly wise, cows know that loss
is our only measure, expellation a passing pleasure.

# Call of the corncrake

There is a tip of forever
in the wait for the cut
when you fly low on rufous wings
and call out your court.

Crane-necked, we hear you
rattle through grass
hoping to mate before meadows
are sheared.

A line that might stop.
No crex comes back
before the machine
grinds in the gap.

What sight is right?
We hope to spy
while you scour the meadow,
*high beak, high eye.*

# The same people living in the same place

i

the first mistake was we believed our own publicity
we were gone and there was no finding us
not through protest not via mothers crying on TV
not through the spiel of indignation when elections loom –
we were gone so far from the seat of power that
this is what they call 'disappeared'
we held ourselves quietly, with dignity we thought
though there was no-one to see, we waited
as a chip waits for a lucky draw,
as the back end of an argument waits for *the reveal*
we waited, until we almost forgot ourselves,
until the hum and the haw of prevarication
was the rhythm it seemed of the seasons.
Will we be left in the lime slide of time
and what will they call us then?

ii

Hell is an island of too many horizons.
A book called *Enquire within about everything*
has got to be framed by the devil.
The first ink drawing of the man with the longest nails in the world.
He cannot change his clothes, his nephews must help him to eat.

An overview of human teeth, separated by race,
herbivore apes on a sliding bar of comparison.
Twenty seven varieties of sausage made from offal,
none including ground chicken feet.

*Oh for the curlicue of an ornate majuscule.*
*Ah to feel a cursive stroke of light.*

Here is the curl in N for *New Ireland*
Here is a list of the least important deaths.

# I was born in a will o' the wisp

came like a twist of the wise to rouse and sunder.
I am the seer you keep at bay, the shadow over your eye.
My might is my slightness, my strength is my veil
the way I catch your wish for the real
with my curling truth on your fingers and toes, in the whorl of your ear –
the conjure of honour, the vision of tribute, I'm there.
They think we're a light that breeds in the ghosting field
to darken the tree-held night
but we're not, we're a smoulder, ash with a centre of roar,
we bide our time while you grow in debt and get older.

When they gather in halls that are named for the money
and they call for our end and muster an army
against what might happen if they upped and entered us
then we are scared –
especially of the dismantlers, they do it so well,
so fast it's the trick of conjuring nil; you don't see what is gone.
Was there nothing there?

When one of you names us and knows our intention
we draw you into our inkling lair, the other dimension
and we sing together the song of no nation
that will prink and spindle the future of wish
the future of wisp at the centre of will.

I was born in a will o' the wisp
and I live here still.

# Gatherer

Where is the morel in these woods?
We keep their secret
knowing they might spoil.
You have to be out early on the hill
to feel the pleat of fleshly curl,
to know they leave no mark.
Plucked from the low rill
turned cleanly out of the dark,
If we do not gather them, who will?

'Periwinkles': Fianna Fáil is the name of the political party often rendered with the subtitle 'the republican party'. It was founded by Éamonn De Valera (called 'Dev' in this poem) and other opponents of the 1921 treaty with the British government.

'Ravens': *Ruaile buaile* from Gaelic (but also used in Hiberno-English) means tumult, commotion or ruction, sometimes with a connotation of celebration.

# Acknowledgements

Acknowledgements are due to the editors of the following journals in which some of these poems or versions of them appeared:
*Asymptote, Magma, Poetry Ireland Review, The Hopkins Review, New Hibernia Review, Communion Magazine, The Stinging Fly, Southword, Forage, The Irish Times, The Ulster Tatler, Cyphers, About Place Journal, Connotation Press – The Poet's Congeries, Tremble – the University of Canberra International Poetry Prize Anthology 2016.*

'Flora' and 'The longing of the bees' were published in *The Stony Thursday Book* 2014 edited by Peter Sirr.

'I was born in a will o' the wisp' appeared in *I live in Michael Hartnett* edited by James Lawlor (Revival Press, 2013).

'Ravens' was included in *Berryman's Fate: a centenary celebration* edited by Philip Coleman (Arlen House, 2014).

'Origin of the mimeo' and 'Camouflage' appear in the Troubles Archive of Artworks (http://www.troublesarchive.com/).

'The same people living in the same place' appeared in the St. Patrick's Day special issue of *The Stinging Fly: In the Wake of the Rising* drawn from *The Stinging Fly* issue 33, Vol 2 edited by Sean O'Reilly (Solas Nua/Stinging Fly, 2016). This poem was also recorded for The Poetry Programme, RTE radio.

'Framed' was awarded the Oxford Brookes International Poetry Prize, 2016.

Grateful thanks to those who read some of this work at an early stage, particularly Paul Farley and Tony Sharpe of Lancaster University, Jean O'Brien, Seamus Cashman and Katie Donovan. Special thanks are due to my husband Kevin, and our children Amy, Luke and Eoin who collectively make this work possible.

## About the author

Siobhán Campbell was born in Dublin. Her collections of poetry are *Cross-Talk* (Seren), *The Permanent Wave* and *The Cold that Burns* (Blackstaff Press) and chapbooks *That water speaks in tongues* (Templar) and *Darwin Among the Machines* (Rack Press). She is co-editor with Nessa O'Mahony of *Eavan Boland: Inside History*, a book of critical and creative responses (Arlen House/Syracuse University Press) and critical work appears in *Making Integral: the poetry of Richard Murphy* (CUP) and in *The Portable Poetry Workshop* (Palgrave). In 2016 she was awarded the Oxford Brookes International Poetry Prize which follows awards in the Templar Poetry Prize and the National and Troubadour International competitions. Siobhan is on faculty in the Dept. of English, The Open University where she is part of the team developing curriculum in the MA, Creative Writing. Widely published in the USA, UK and Ireland her work is     regularly anthologised including in the *Forward Book of Poetry* (Faber), *Women's Work: Modern Women Poets writing in English* (Seren), *Identity Parade: New British and Irish Poets* (Bloodaxe), *The Field Day Anthology of Irish Literature* (NYU Press) and *The Golden Shovel Anthology: Honouring Gwendolyn Brooks* (UAP). She has broadcast her work on BBC and RTE radio and given several readings in  Ireland, the UK and US/Canada.

www.siobhancampbell.com

## Well chosen words

Seren is an independent publisher with a wide-ranging list which includes poetry, fiction, biography, art, translation, criticism and history. Many of our books and authors have been on longlists and shortlists for – or won – major literary prizes, among them the Costa Award, the Jerwood Fiction Uncovered Prize, the Man Booker, the Desmond Elliott Prize, The Writers' Guild Award, Forward Prize and TS Eliot Prize.

At the heart of our list is a beautiful poem, a good story told well or an idea or history presented interestingly or provocatively. We're international in authorship and readership though our roots are here in Wales (Seren means Star in Welsh), where we prove that writers from a small country with an intricate culture have a worldwide relevance.

Our aim is to publish work of the highest literary and artistic merit that also succeeds commercially in a competitive, fast changing environment. You can help us achieve this goal by reading more of our books – available from all good bookshops and increasingly as e-books. You can also buy them at 20% discount from our website, and get monthly updates about forthcoming titles, readings, launches and other news about Seren and the authors we publish.

www.serenbooks.com